ROLL-ON Lip Gloss STUDIO

by the editors of Klutz

KLUTZ®

KLUTZ® creates activity books and other great stuff for kids ages 3 to 103. We began our corporate life in 1977 in a garage we shared with a Chevrolet Impala. Although we've outgrown that first office, Klutz galactic headquarters is still staffed entirely by real human beings. For those of you who collect mission statements, here's ours:

CREATE WONDERFUL THINGS · BE GOOD · HAVE FUN

Roller applicators, flowers, crystals, sticker sheet, and flavor drops made in China. All other components, Taiwan. 85

WRITE US
We would love to hea[r] your comments regardi[ng] this or any of our book[s].
KLUTZ®
557 Broadway
New York, NY 10012
thefolks@klutz.com

Distributed in Australia by
Scholastic Australia Ltd
PO Box 579
Gosford, NSW
Australia 2250

Distributed in Canada by
Scholastic Canada Ltd
604 King Street West
Toronto, Ontario
Canada M5V 1E1

Distributed in Hong Kong by
Scholastic Hong Kong Ltd
Suites 2001-2,
Top Glory Tower
262 Gloucester Road
Causeway Bay, Hong Kong

978-1-338-35521-5
4 1 5 8 5 7 0 8 8 8

Ingredients/Ingrédients
lip gloss base/brillant à lèvres: Glycerin, Aloe Barbadensis, Aqua/Water/Eau, Carbomer, Triethanolamine, Phenoxyethanol, Caprylyl Glycol

peachy flavor/parfum de pêche: 1,1-propanediol, Gamma-Undecalactone, Gamma-Decalactone, Delta-Decalactone, Linalool, Delta-Dodecanolactone, 3-Hexenol

sequins/paillettes: polyethylene terephthalate, acrylates copolymer, aluminum

Safety Information
Use only as directed; Follow all directions in the book.
Patch test for sensitivity first. Do not use on broken or irritated skin.
If components are swallowed, seek medical advice immediately. In case of contact with the eyes, rinse well with water.
Discontinue use if irritation occurs. If irritation persists, consult a physician.

Sécurité renseignements
Respecter les instructions d'emploi; Suivre toutes les directives du livre. Effectuez d'abord un test cutané en cas de reaction. Ne pas utilizer sur la peau échorchée ou irritée. Si des composants sont avalés, consulter immédiatement un médecin. En cas de contact avec les yeux, bien rincer avec de l'eau. Cesser d'utiliser ce produit en cas d'irritation cutanée. Consulter un médecin si l'irritation persiste.

CONTENTS

WHAT YOU GET

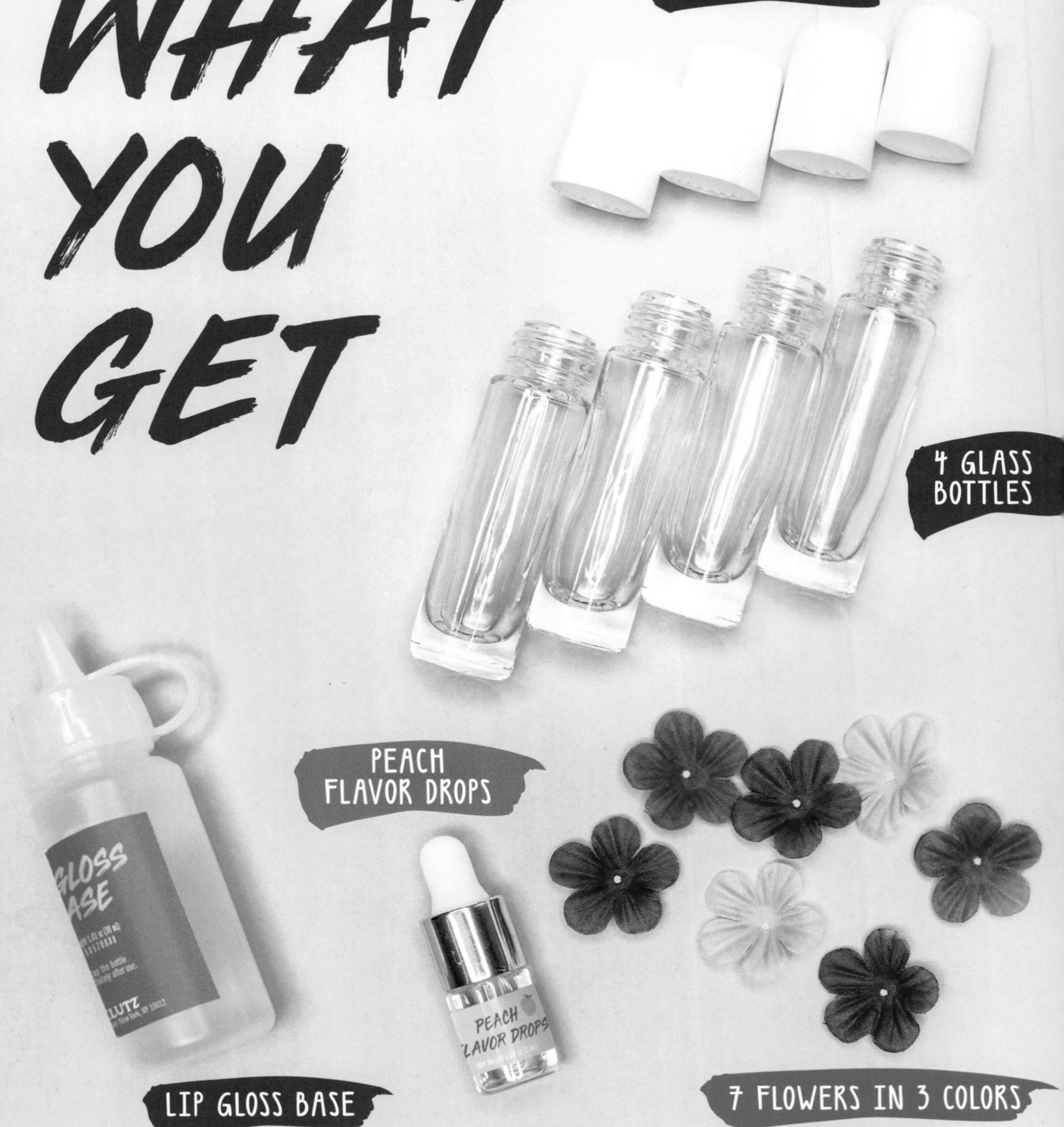

4 BOTTLE CAPS
4 GLASS BOTTLES
PEACH FLAVOR DROPS
GLOSS BASE
KLUTZ
PEACH FLAVOR DROPS
LIP GLOSS BASE
7 FLOWERS IN 3 COLORS

HOLOGRAPHIC SEQUINS

4 ROLLERS

STICKERS

CRYSTALS IN 3 COLORS

LIP GLOSS STAND

For the DIY recipes in this book, you'll need to gather these ingredients from your kitchen:

- ☐ Mixing bowl
- ☐ Microwave-safe bowl
- ☐ Spoon
- ☐ Whisk or fork
- ☐ Oven mitts
- ☐ Small containers for storage
- ☐ Coconut oil
- ☐ Pink sanding sugar
- ☐ Rose water
- ☐ Vegetable oil
- ☐ Sugar
- ☐ Dried tea leaves
- ☐ Rainbow sprinkles
- ☐ Shea butter
- ☐ Beeswax pastilles
- ☐ Ice tray (silicone works best)

Try to upcycle things like old lip balm containers, small jam jars, and mint tins. Get creative!

GLOSS IS BOSS

Never without your trusty wand of gloss, tube of balm, or jar of salve? You're not alone!

WHAT'S THE DEAL WITH LIP BALM ANYWAY?

Turns out, the skin on your lips is unique. Your skin produces oil (which helps protect against germs and bacteria) everywhere except your lips. Add cold and windy weather to the mix, and your lips could really use an extra layer of protection.

Even though you can buy loads of lip gloss at a store, it's really fun to design your own! In this kit, you'll find lab-tested ingredients, a clear gloss base made from glycerin and aloe, faux flowers, and sparkly crystals to customize a lip gloss that's just your style.

SAFETY INFO

★ This book is full of fun beauty recipes for your lips. But if any recipe stings, burns, itches, or causes you pain in any way, stop using it immediately and ask an adult for help. If you are sensitive or allergic to any ingredients, your grown-up assistant can help you find substitutes. Make sure to keep your supplies and fabulous finished beauty products away from babies and pets.

★ Your lip gloss will be safe and fun to wear, but remember a little goes a long way.

★ Always practice safe kitchen skills. Some of the recipes in this book require microwaving and pouring hot liquid. A grown-up assistant should always handle any heating equipment. Store your finished products in plastic containers, not glass, to prevent breaking.

MESSAGE IN A BOTANICAL

Botanicals (plants and flowers) are ingredients in perfume, makeup, and medicine, but did you know they also send secret messages? The language of flowers is called floriography (floor-ee-OG-ruh-fee), and has been practiced all over the world. It became especially popular in the British Victorian Era (1837–1901). Victorians studied floriography to figure out the perfect flower to give someone according to its meaning.

HERE ARE SOME EXAMPLES OF FLOWERS AND WHAT THEY MEAN. WHICH WOULD YOU CHOOSE TO GIVE TO YOUR BEST FRIENDS?

CHAMOMILE
energy

CHERRY BLOSSOM
intelligence

HONEYSUCKLE
generosity

JASMINE
friendship, grace

LAVENDER
loyalty and gratitude

PINK ROSE
happiness

IRIS
wisdom

LILY
sweetness

DAFFODIL
joy

Find Your Flower

SLEEPOVER FUN!

Baking cookies

Scary movies

CUPCAKE TOPPING

Chocolate frosting

Rainbow sprinkles

Gummy worms

I'D RATHER SPOT...

A rainbow

A shooting star

ONE DAY I'LL WRITE...

Cartoons

MUST-HAVE MUSIC

Poems

Mystery books

Loud pop

Chill beats

FORGET-ME-NOT
Witty and thoughtful, forget-me-nots represent loyalty and intelligence.

PINK ROSE
Always expressive, the pink rose is for silly jokesters who love pranks and making others laugh.

LAVENDER
A calming, relaxing presence and a popular garden flower, lavender symbolizes an important friend who makes others feel special.

9

FLOWER POWER GLOSS

Add a boost to your bottle with some pretty petals! Choose the ones that fit your personality (page 9), or stack the pink first, then the purple and blue for an ombré effect.

WHAT YOU'LL NEED

- Glass bottle
- 3 flowers:
  1 blue,
  1 purple,
  1 pink
- Lip gloss base
- ☐ Peach flavor drops
- ☐ Chopstick or pencil (optional)
- ☐ Roller
- ☐ Bottle cap

1 Place the bottle upright on a clean work surface.

2 Fold the blue flower and push it through the opening. Repeat with the purple and pink flowers. You can use a chopstick or pencil to make sure they are in the right place.

3 Tilt the glass bottle on an angle, and insert the tip of the gloss base into the opening. Slowly add the base until there's ½ inch (13 mm) of space left at the top.

4 Stand the glass bottle right side up, and use the dropper to squeeze out two drops of peach flavor drops.

5 Add the roller. (Get an adult to help you if this is tricky.) Then screw on the cap. Flip the bottle upside down to mix in the flavor.

PRO TIP

To get your gloss going, use your fingertip to move the rollerball around.

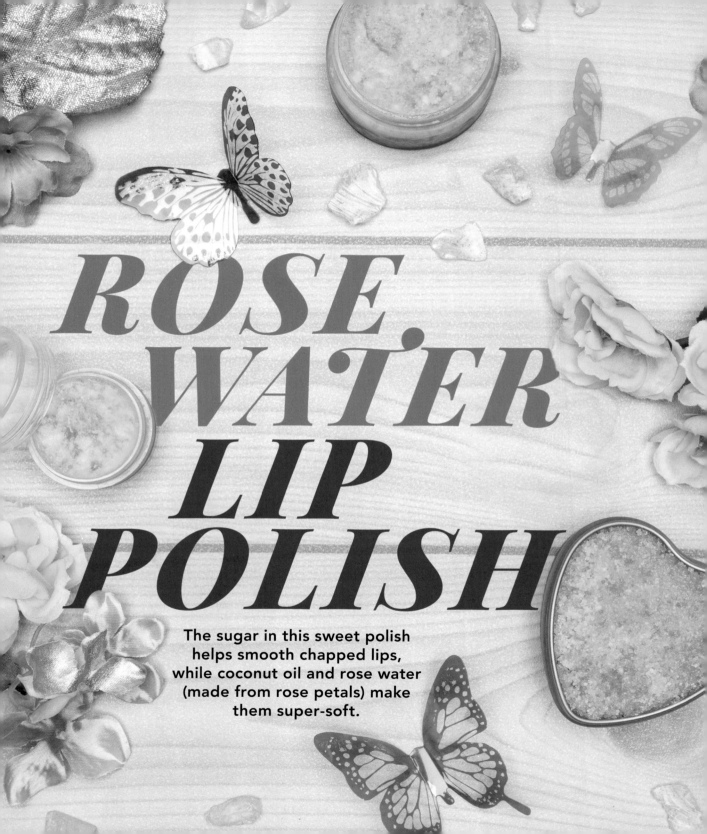

ROSE WATER LIP POLISH

The sugar in this sweet polish helps smooth chapped lips, while coconut oil and rose water (made from rose petals) make them super-soft.

WHAT YOU'LL NEED

- ☐ 1 tablespoon (15 mL) sugar (refined or raw)
- ☐ 2 teaspoons (10 mL) pink sanding sugar (optional, to make the scrub pink!)
- ☐ 1 teaspoon (5 mL) rose water
- ☐ 1 teaspoon (5 mL) coconut oil
- ☐ Mixing bowl
- ☐ Whisk or fork
- ☐ Small airtight storage container

① Add the coconut oil and rose water in the bowl.

PRO TIP
Rose water can be found at the drugstore or at the grocery store in the international section.

② Mix them together with a whisk or fork.

PRO TIP
Look for pink sanding sugar at your grocery store or local craft store, in the cake decorating aisle.

③ Add both kinds of sugar and mix to combine.

④ To use the scrub, apply 1 teaspoon of the scrub to your lips and massage in a circular motion for 30 seconds. Then wash it off with water.

⑤ Keep the rest in an airtight storage container, like a small jar, in the fridge and use it for up to two weeks.

CRYSTAL CLARITY QUIZ

While we aren't using actual rocks in the lip gloss, the sparkly nuggets in this kit look like stones that some people believe have special energies. Check out these colorful crystals, and take the quiz to find the one for you!

AVENTURINE
risk-taking

CITRINE
confidence

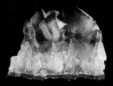

AMETHYST
relaxation

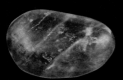

LAPIS LAZULI
imagination

FLOURITE
mental clarity

HEMATITE
focus

CARNELIAN
ambition

AMAZONITE
positivity

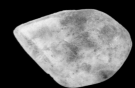

SUNSTONE
creativity

Which crystal matches your personality?

START HERE

SUPERPOWER

- Flying
- Reading minds

RELAX MODE ⟶ A good book

- Painting nails
- TV marathon

TAKE A TRIP

Mountain meadow

- New city

BEST PET

DREAM JOB ⟶ Rock star

- Chameleon
- Giraffe

- Astronaut
- Video game designer

ROSE QUARTZ
ose quartz is the best emotional healer. Calm and soothing, it encourages self-trust and self-orth, drawing out negativity and placing it with love and positivity.

AZURITE
Bold and brilliant, azurite is used for focus and transformation. With powerful energy, azurite challenges old ideas, gives a sense of bravery and adventure, and promotes new experiences.

MALACHITE
This crystal carries the deep green of nature. The stone of inner strength, malachite brings energy and new growth, and encourages wisdom and creativity.

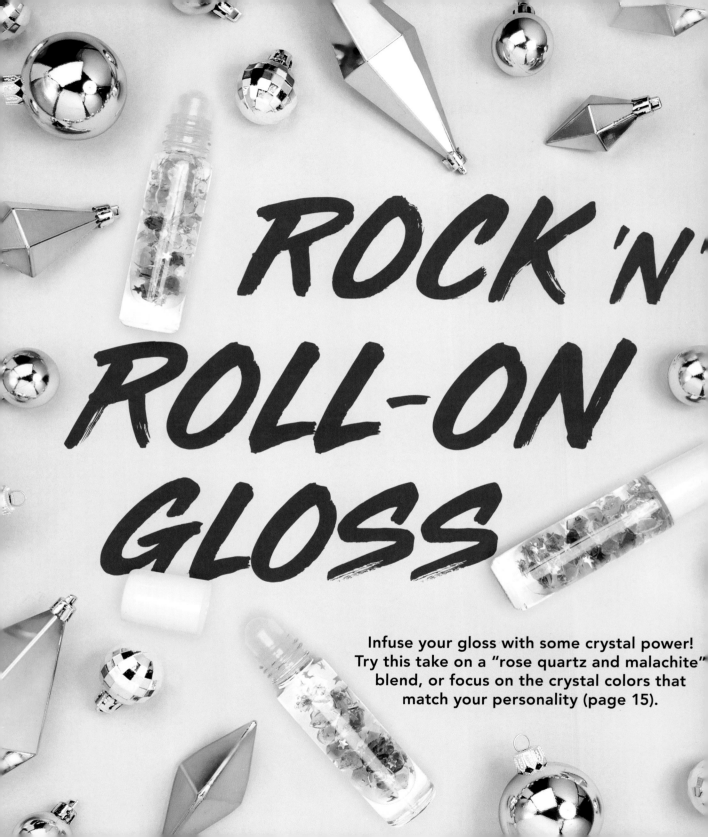

ROCK 'N' ROLL-ON GLOSS

Infuse your gloss with some crystal power! Try this take on a "rose quartz and malachite" blend, or focus on the crystal colors that match your personality (page 15).

WHAT YOU'LL NEED

- Glass bottle
- 10 pink crystals
- 10 green crystals
- 5 blue crystals
- Lip gloss base
- ☐ Pinch of holographic sequins
- ☐ Peach flavor drops
- ☐ Roller
- ☐ Bottle cap

1 Place the glass bottle upright on a clean work surface.

One by one, drop the crystals into the bottle.

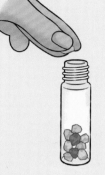

2 Take a pinch of holographic sequins and sprinkle it into the bottle.

3 Tilt the glass bottle on an angle, and insert the tip of the base into the opening. Slowly add the base until there's ½ inch (13 mm) of space left at the top.

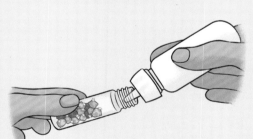

4 Stand the glass bottle right side up, and squeeze out two drops of peach flavor drops.

PRO TIP

Adding holographic sequins can be messy. Make it easy by cutting the corner of an envelope or piece of mail to make a funnel with a tiny opening at the bottom. Put the narrow opening into the bottle mouth and sprinkle glitter in the funnel.

5 Press the roller in. (Get an adult to help you if this is tricky!) Then screw on the cap, and flip the bottle upside down to mix in the flavor.

SUGAR CRYSTAL BUFF

Would you believe the frosting on your cupcake is made of tiny crystals? If you look at sugar under a microscope, you'll see that each granule is actually a crystal!

WHAT YOU'LL NEED

- ☐ Mixing bowl
- ☐ 1 tablespoon (15mL) turbinado sugar
- ☐ 2 teaspoons (10 mL) vegetable oil
- ☐ Whisk
- ☐ Small airtight storage container

PRO TIP

Turbinado sugar has especially big crystals, so it makes a great crystal scrub, but you can use brown, regular cane, or any colorful sanding sugar if it's handy.

1 Add the sugar to the bowl.

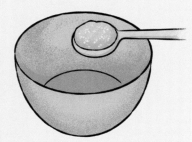

2 Pour the oil into the bowl and mix with a whisk until it's combined with the sugar.

3 Apply a little bit to your lips with your fingers and massage in a circular motion for 30 seconds. Then wash it off with water.

4 Store any leftovers in an airtight storage container and keep it in the fridge. Use it any time you need a little crystal magic for up to two weeks!

safety bit

If it's been more than two weeks, clean out your jar and replace it with a fresh scrub!

NIGHT TIME GALAXY GLOSS

Lip shine with a cosmic twist? It's totally out-of-this-world!
Create an enchanted gloss by filling your bottle with
evening hues flecked with stars.

WHAT YOU'LL NEED

- Glass bottle
- 1 blue flower
- 1 purple flower
- Chopstick or pencil (optional)
- 13 blue crystals
- Pinch of holographic sequins
- ☐ Lip gloss base
- ☐ Peach flavor drops
- ☐ Roller
- ☐ Bottle cap

1 Place the glass bottle upright on a clean work surface.

Fold the flowers and push them into the bottle. You can use a chopstick or pencil to make sure they are in the right place.

2 Add the crystals one by one.

3 Sprinkle a tiny bit of holographic sequins into the bottle.

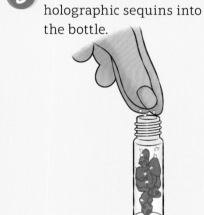

4 Tilt the glass bottle on an angle, and insert the tip of the base into the opening. Slowly add the base until there's ½ inch (13 mm) of space left at the top.

5 Stand the glass bottle right side up, and squeeze out two drops of peach flavor drops.

6 Press the roller in. (Get an adult to help you if this is tricky!) Then screw on the cap, and flip the bottle upside down to mix in the flavor.

SOOTHING SIGN SCRUB

Astrologists believe that your life is affected by your astrological sign (how the stars were grouped in the sky on your birthday). Each of the 12 signs belong to one of four elements: fire, water, air, and earth. For this therapeutic scrub, mix in the tea leaves that best match your "element."

WHAT YOU'LL NEED

- ☐ 1 tablespoon (15 mL) sugar
- ☐ 1/2 teaspoon (2.5 mL) dried tea leaves
- ☐ 1/2 tablespoon (7.5 mL) vegetable oil
- ☐ Spoon
- ☐ Small airtight storage container

1 Add the sugar, the tea leaves, and vegetable oil to the mixing bowl. Stir with a spoon to combine.

2 Use your finger to scoop up some of the scrub and massage the scrub onto your lips for 30 seconds. Rinse off with warm water.

3 If you have extra scrub, keep it in a small airtight container and store the scrub in the fridge for up to two weeks.

AIR
Aquarius
(January 20–February 18)

Gemini
(May 21–June 20)

Libra
(September 23–October 22)

MINT TEA
Your curiosity and intelligence pairs perfectly with cooling, crisp mint tea.

WATER
Pisces
(February 19–March 20)

Cancer
(June 21–July 22)

Scorpio
(October 23–November 21)

EARL GREY TEA
The blend of citrus and black tea brings balance to your creative and artistic sides.

FIRE
Aries
(March 21–April 19)

Leo
(July 23–August 22)

Sagittarius
(November 22–December 21)

CHAI TEA
Warm spices like cinnamon and cardamom in chai tea feed the energy of your fiery spirit.

EARTH
Taurus
(April 20–May 20)

Virgo
(August 23–September 22)

Capricorn
(December 22–January 19)

GREEN TEA
Strengthen your hard-working nature with bold and bright green tea.

SWEET DREAMS NIGHT MASK

Honey and coconut oil are both expert moisturizers. Apply this mask before bed and wake up with super-smooth lips.

WHAT YOU'LL NEED

☐ 2 teaspoons (10 mL) coconut oil
☐ 2 teaspoons (10 mL) honey
☐ Mixing bowl
☐ Whisk
☐ Small airtight storage container

1 Add 2 teaspoons (10 mL) of coconut oil to the bowl.

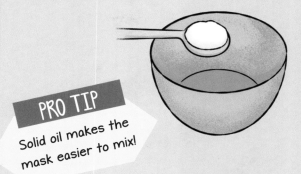

PRO TIP
Solid oil makes the mask easier to mix!

2 Add the honey and stir it with a whisk until the ingredients are combined.

3 Using your finger, apply a layer of the mask to your lips before you go to sleep.

4 Store the mask in a small airtight container and keep it in the fridge. Reapply it if your lips need extra conditioning!

safety bit
If it's been more than two weeks, clean out your jar and replace it with a fresh mask!

UNICORN MAGIC GLOSS

Shiny, sparkly, and super-colorful, this gloss combo helps bring out your inner unicorn!

WHAT YOU'LL NEED

- Glass bottle
- 7 pink crystals
- 7 green crystals
- 1 purple flower
- 1 pink flower
- Chopstick or pencil (optional)
- ☐ Pinch of holographic sequins
- ☐ Lip gloss base
- ☐ Peach flavor drops
- ☐ Roller
- ☐ Bottle cap

1 Remove the cap and place the glass bottle upright on a clean work surface.

Fold one flower and push it through the opening. Repeat with the other flower. You can use a chopstick or pencil to make sure they are in place.

2 Add the crystals to the bottle one by one.

3 Sprinkle a pinch of holographic sequins in the bottle.

4 Tilt the bottle on an angle and insert the tip of the base into the opening. Slowly add the base until there's ½ inch (13 mm) of space left at the top.

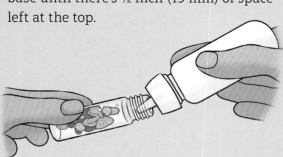

5 Add two drops of peach flavor drops before you put the roller and the bottle cap on. (Have an adult help if it's tricky.)

RAINBOW SPRINKLE BALM

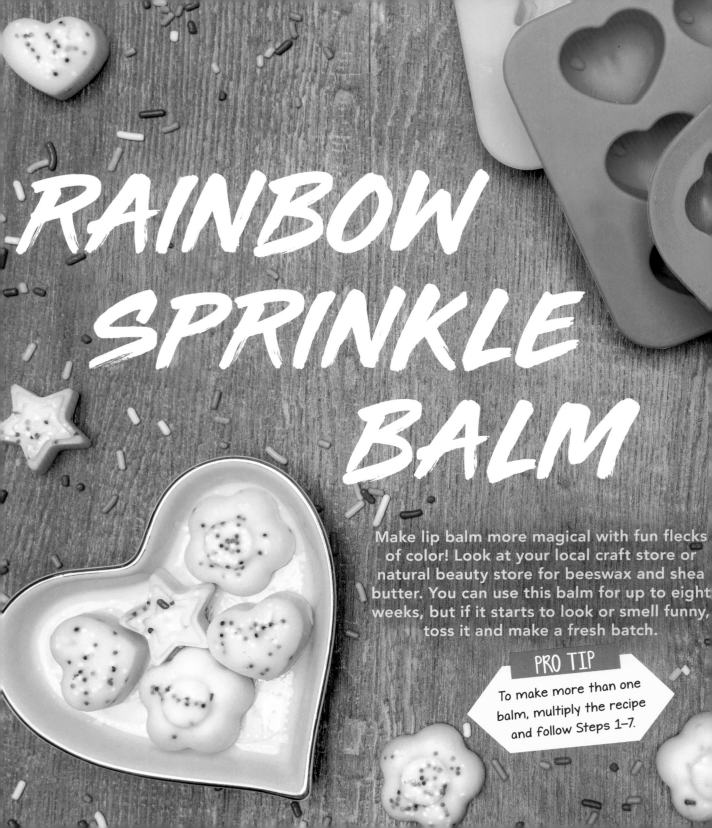

Make lip balm more magical with fun flecks of color! Look at your local craft store or natural beauty store for beeswax and shea butter. You can use this balm for up to eight weeks, but if it starts to look or smell funny, toss it and make a fresh batch.

PRO TIP

To make more than one balm, multiply the recipe and follow Steps 1–7.

WHAT YOU'LL NEED

- 1 tablespoon (15 mL) beeswax pastilles
- 1 tablespoon (15 mL) shea butter
- 1 teaspoon (5 mL) coconut oil
- 1/2 teaspoon (2.5 mL) rainbow sprinkles
- ☐ Microwave-safe measuring cup
- ☐ Whisk
- ☐ Ice-cube tray (silicone works best)
- ☐ Small airtight storage container

1 Using your finger, coat the inside of the ice mold with a tiny bit of coconut oil.

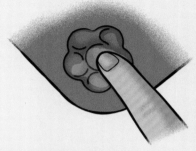

2 Add a layer of sprinkles on the inside of the mold. They should stick to the coconut oil, but you can adjust them with your finger so they make an even layer.

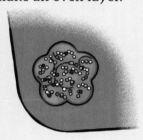

3 Add the beeswax and the shea butter to the measuring cup.

4 With the help of an adult, microwave it for 20 seconds. Then check to see if it has melted. If you need to melt it more, make sure you only microwave it for short, 20-second bursts.

5 Stir the mixture with a whisk to mix and melt any clumps. Add the coconut oil and keep mixing to combine everything.

6 Pour the melted mixture into the mold until it almost reaches the top.

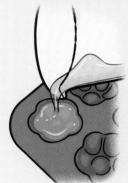

7 Put the tray in the freezer for one hour. Once they've hardened, pop the balms out of the tray. Use the balm to add some rainbow flair to your lips.

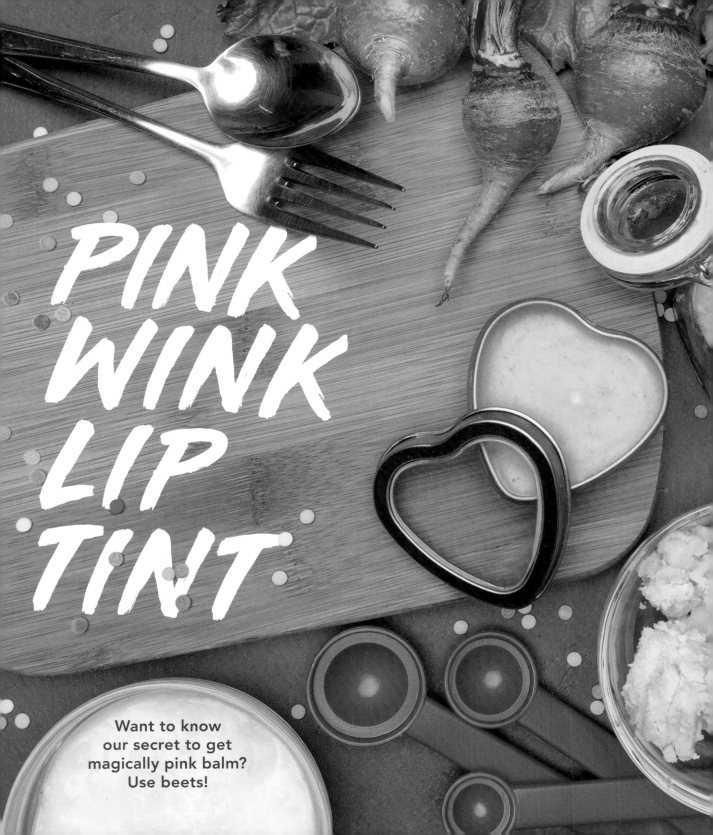

PINK WINK LIP TINT

Want to know our secret to get magically pink balm? Use beets!

WHAT YOU'LL NEED

- [ ] 2 teaspoons (10 mL) coconut oil
- [ ] 2 tablespoons (30 mL) shea butter
- [ ] 1/2 teaspoon (2.5 mL) beet juice
- [ ] Mixing bowl
- [ ] Whisk
- [ ] Spoon
- [ ] Small airtight storage container

PRO TIP

You can find beet juice at your grocery store, or use a little bit of the liquid from canned beets.

1 Combine the coconut oil, shea butter, and beet juice in a small microwave-safe bowl and stir together with a whisk.

2 If mixing everything is tricky, put the bowl in the fridge for 30 minutes.

30

3 Take the mix out of the fridge and continue to stir until the ingredients are combined.

4 Spoon the mix into the airtight storage container. Now you're ready for a hint of tint!

safety bit After two weeks, clean out your container and replace it with a fresh tint.

GLAM DISPLAY

Once you've designed your lip gloss, it's time to give your bottles a super-cool stand!

1 You can find the display hidden in the cardboard insert tray! To make a pretty place for your gloss, punch out the display piece and set it in front of you with the dark side facing up.

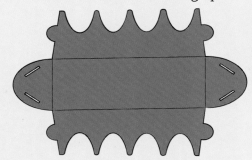

2 Fold the display along the score lines with the pink and purple sides facing out.

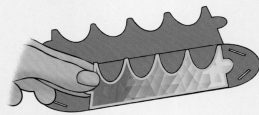

3 There are little tabs o the corners of each lo edge. Fold the short s inward so their slots over the tabs.

4 Once the sides are in place, the base of each lip gloss bottle can fit snugly in the display.

Decorate the caps, bottles, and display with cute stickers!